Gravity

Don Herweck

Consultant

Michelle Alfonsi
Engineer, Southern California
Aerospace Industry

Image Credits: pp.2–3 Team Sandtastic; p.8 (left)
age fotostock Spain, S.L./Alamy; pp.12–13 Cultura
Creative/Alamy; pp.5–7, 11, 13, 25 (illustrations) Tim
Bradley; pp.18–19 Gravity Glue; backcover, pp.4–5
(background), 8 (background), 16 (left), 17 (top),
20–25 (background) iStock; pp.28–29 (illustrations)
Janelle Bell-Martin; pp.17 (bottom right), 18 (bottom
left) NASA; p.4 Isis Sousa; p.20 Chase Studio/Science
Source; p.21 (both top) GIPhotoStock/Science
Source; pp.26–27 Paul Wootton/Science Source;
p.7 (top) Photo Researchers/Science Source;
all other images from Shutterstock.

Library of Congress Cataloging-in-Publication Data

Herweck, Don, author.
  Gravity / Don Herweck.
    pages cm
  Summary: "If you throw a ball, it will soar through the
air and then fall with a thump to the floor—thanks to
gravity! Gravity makes life possible for all of us. Without
gravity we would all float into space. So next time you
do—well, anything—thank gravity."—Provided by
publisher.
  Audience: K to grade 3.
  Includes index.
  ISBN 978-1-4807-4644-2 (pbk.)
  ISBN 978-1-4807-5088-3 (ebook)
  1. Gravity—Juvenile literature. I. Title.
QC178.H395 2015
531.5—dc23
                                    2014034268

Teacher Created Materials

5301 Oceanus Drive
Huntington Beach, CA 92649-1030
http://www.tcmpub.com
ISBN 978-1-4807-4644-2
© 2015 Teacher Created Materials, Inc.
Printed in Malaysia
Thumbprints.042019

Table of Contents

What Goes Up Must Come Down

No one can deny the power of gravity. We can't see gravity. But we feel its effects every day. Imagine what life would be like without it. Trees, buildings, and cars wouldn't stay on the ground. Even the air we breathe would float away!

Gravity is the **force** that pulls us toward Earth. It attracts objects toward each other. In fact, all objects are attracted to the gravity of other objects. That includes Earth and the people who live on it. Earth pulls on us, and we pull on Earth. But what's behind this force?

Finding Forces

Sir Isaac Newton was a scientist in the 17th and 18th centuries. Newton discovered three laws, or rules, that explain the way objects move. One of these laws tells us how a force such as gravity, acts on an object.

Without gravity, our lives would be very different!

The Fabric of Space

Space is all around us. We move up, down, backward, forward, and sideways in it. We can't see it, but space is everywhere.

Space is like a piece of fabric that never ends and stretches in every direction. Objects in space curve the area around them. Think of a tennis ball resting on a piece of fabric. The fabric bends under the ball. And a larger object, such as a bowling ball, pulls on the fabric even more. A small marble on the fabric would fall toward a larger ball. Gravity works the same way. It occurs when objects curve the space around them. And just like the balls on the fabric, objects in space fall toward each other.

Going the Distance

The closer two objects are, the more they are attracted to each other. When objects are farther apart, the effects of gravity are weaker.

Deep Thoughts

Albert Einstein lived in the 19th and 20th centuries. He thought deeply about what might cause gravity. He developed the idea that gravity occurs when objects curve the space around them.

More Mass = More Gravity

Gravity varies depending on an object's mass. Mass is the amount of **matter** in an object. Matter is what all things are made of. It's easy to confuse mass with weight. But they are different. Weight is the force of gravity on an object's mass. When you step on a scale, Earth's gravity pulls you down. This puts pressure on the scale. The more you weigh, the more the scale is pushed. The number on the scale is called *weight*.

Gravity is the force pulling this apple down.

An object's mass never changes. But an object's weight changes based on where it is in the universe. If an object is somewhere with lots of gravity, such as Earth, it weighs more. If it is somewhere with less gravity, such as the moon, it weighs less.

Measuring the Force

Hundreds of years ago, Newton discovered gravity as a force that can be measured. Today, scientists honor him by measuring the force of gravity in newtons (N). Just like length can be measured in feet, inches, or yards, gravity can be measured in newtons.

en, bigger objects have more mass. But
n't always related to size. Very small
can have a lot of mass. And something
ge might have less mass than something
A simple example is a golf ball that has
ass than a beach ball. It's smaller, but
nore stuff packed into the space.

cts with more mass curve more space.
ve more gravity. Objects with less mass
gravity. Just think about the bowling
the marble. The marble falls toward the
ball in the fabric of space. It's the same
ple and Earth. People have less mass
th has. So Earth's gravity is greater.
e pulled toward Earth. That's what
rom floating off into space.

To the Moon!

Space travel was only made possible
by knowing how gravity works. Once
scientists learned the strength of Earth's
gravity, they figured out the force needed
to overcome it. To escape Earth's gravity, a
space shuttle must travel 40,234 kilometers
per hour (25,000 miles per hour)!

What's Weighing You Down?

Every **celestial** (suh-LES-chuhl) body has a different mass. So the force of gravity changes on each.

	MOON	EARTH	JUPITER
Mass of the celestial body	The moon's mass is 81 times smaller than Earth's.	Standard	Jupiter's mass is 300 times greater than Earth's.
Weight of a person	An average adult would weigh 12 kilograms (26 pounds) on the moon, about the same as a toddler on Earth.	An average adult on Earth weighs 70 kg (154 lb.).	An average adult would weigh 165 kg (364 lb.) on Jupiter, about the same as a tiger on Earth.
What it feels like	Your muscles would get soft and weak if you stayed too long because they wouldn't have to work very hard to keep you standing.	It feels like home.	You would feel like you were being crushed into the ground. Your muscles would have to work very hard to keep you standing.
How high can you jump?	On the moon, most people would be able to jump 550 centimeters (18 feet).	On Earth, most people can jump 91 cm (3 ft.).	On Jupiter, most people would be able to jump 0 cm (0 ft.).

Inertia

Newton discovered that moving objects keep moving. They will keep going and going unless something stops them. And an object at rest, or not moving, stays at rest until something pushes or pulls it. Newton called this law of motion **inertia** (in-UR-shuh).

To move something large, you must have more inertia than the object does. A boulder has a lot of mass. It has so much inertia that there's no way for you to push it even an inch. But a pebble has much less mass. And that means it has less inertia. So you can move it easily with just a finger.

Everything with mass has inertia. Life on Earth has developed some amazing ways to take advantage of it.

When a cat dips its tongue into water, a tiny bit of water sticks to the tip of its tongue.

When a cat pulls its tongue up, the inertia of the water causes a trail of liquid to get pulled up, too.

The cat closes its mouth just before gravity kicks in and sends the water splashing back into the bowl.

Break dancers use the inertia of their swinging legs to spin on their heads!

Inertia and gravity work together on objects. If you throw a ball, it travels in a curved path. Now, imagine what would happen if gravity didn't exist. Inertia would keep the ball moving forward in a straight line. There would be nothing to stop the ball. But in reality, gravity is always acting on the ball. It pulls the ball down. So the ball is always falling. But it's falling in a curved path because inertia pushes it forward.

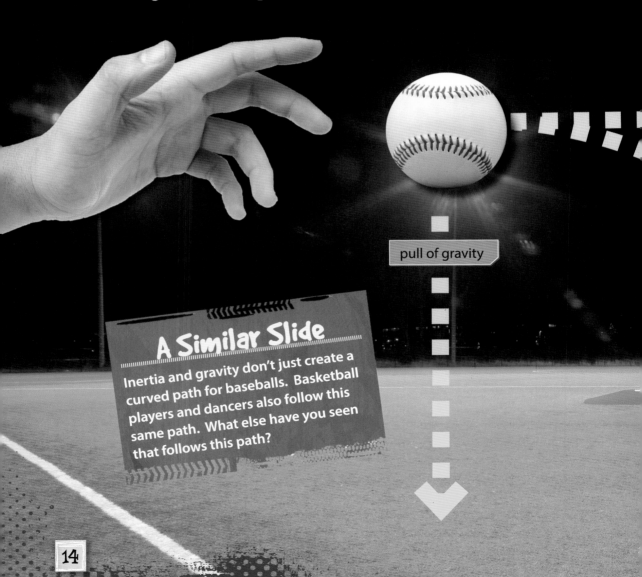

pull of gravity

A Similar Slide

Inertia and gravity don't just create a curved path for baseballs. Basketball players and dancers also follow this same path. What else have you seen that follows this path?

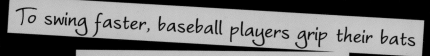

To swing faster, baseball players grip their bats higher up. This reduces inertia and increases bat speed.

inertial path

ball's path

Effects of Gravity

Everything on Earth is attracted to everything else—including Earth! Gravity affects everything from the smallest bug to the tallest skyscraper. Life on Earth has developed in ways that make us feel comfortable. Fighting against the pull of gravity keeps our bones and muscles strong. Gravity even helps carry blood through our bodies. But gravity also affects the planet in bigger ways.

Finding Your Center

Every object has a center of gravity. In a sphere, or round object, the center of gravity is right in the middle. Gravity always pulls objects toward the center. So on a planet, no matter where you are, down is toward the center of the sphere.

The Vomit Comet

It can be hard for astronauts to live in space where there is no gravity. They practice by traveling in special airplanes that give the feeling of floating by traveling up and down very quickly. These planes are called "vomit comets" because they often make people lose their lunch.

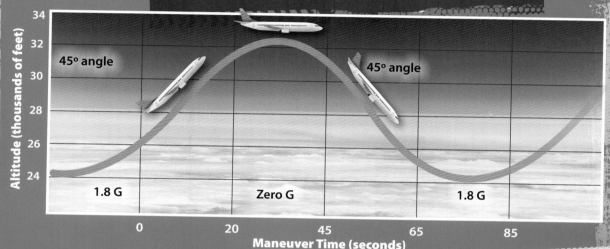

Altitude (thousands of feet)

45° angle — 45° angle

1.8 G — Zero G — 1.8 G

Maneuver Time (seconds)

0   20   45   65   85

At each peak, astronauts feel 25 seconds of weightlessness. As the plane climbs and descends, they feel almost twice the force of gravity.

17

Rock Cycle

Rocks may seem like they have been around forever and are impossible to destroy. But they are constantly changing due to the **rock cycle**. Gravity is one of the forces that drives this change. Everything from a grain of sand to huge canyons feels gravity's effects.

Wind and water break large rocks into small pieces. Gravity pulls loose rock to the ground. If it pulls small rocks off a cliff, they will break into even smaller pieces. Gravity also pulls rocks into volcanoes and underground. Below Earth's surface, heat and gravity's pressure turn rocks into new types of rocks, and the cycle continues.

Rock On!

Scientists use special **satellites** above Earth to see underground. Earth may seem like a perfectly round ball. But these spacecrafts show that Earth's mass changes in places.

Gravity Glue

Try making a rock sculpture using only gravity as the glue. All you need to do is place one rock on top of the other. The possibilities are endless!

Water Cycle

Gravity pulls on large rocks and tiny raindrops, too. The water on Earth has been here for billions of years. The **water cycle** reuses this water every day. Gravity plays an important role in this cycle.

Gravity pulls water from clouds to Earth. When raindrops land on the ground, gravity pulls them downhill. When snow melts, it's also pulled downhill by gravity. Gravity also pulls water through layers of rocks and soil, deep into the ground. Plants use this water to live and grow. As water travels, it may form ponds, lakes, or streams. Gravity pulls water downstream until it reaches the ocean. The water in oceans, ponds, and streams also **evaporates**. It rises into the air. Then, the cycle begins again.

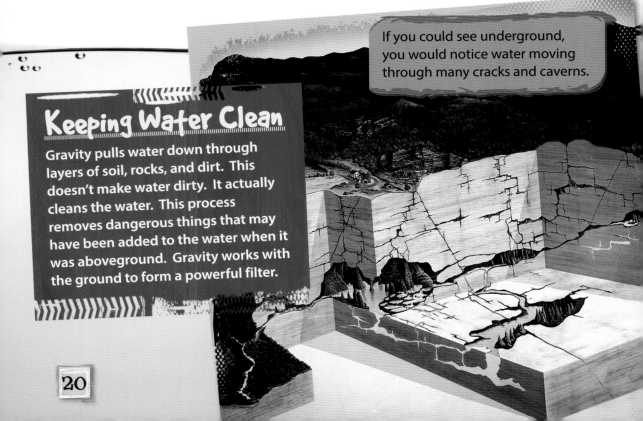

If you could see underground, you would notice water moving through many cracks and caverns.

Keeping Water Clean

Gravity pulls water down through layers of soil, rocks, and dirt. This doesn't make water dirty. It actually cleans the water. This process removes dangerous things that may have been added to the water when it was aboveground. Gravity works with the ground to form a powerful filter.

high tide

low tide

Tides

Have you ever been to the ocean? Sometimes, the water level is high on the shore. This is called a *high tide*. At low tide, the water level seems to shrink, so more of the shore can be seen. The moon's gravity causes this mysterious motion.

The moon's gravity pulls Earth toward it. And the water in Earth's oceans is pulled, too. This pull creates a bulge in the water on both sides of the planet. When the moon is directly overhead, it is high tide. The moon's gravity and Earth's rotation create two high tides and two low tides each day.

In Space

Gravity doesn't just pull things toward Earth. It pulls things together across the universe. Every night, we see the moon **orbiting** Earth. It appears to be circling us. And it is. But in a very real way, it is actually falling toward us.

Without gravity, the moon would have flown off into space a long time ago. Gravity pulls the moon toward Earth. But the moon is still flying through space very quickly. This creates a circular orbit. If the moon were as small as a basketball (or a meteor), it would fall toward Earth and crash. But the moon has plenty of inertia. Inertia and gravity combine to make the moon orbit Earth.

path the moon would naturally take

pull of the moon and Earth on each other

moon

orbit of the moon around Earth

Earth

Microgravity

In outer space, objects appear weightless. Microgravity occurs when the pull of gravity is weak. It's easy to move heavy objects like people, elephants, and even space stations in microgravity.

Look farther out into the solar system. You'll see that gravity has the same effect. Each planet in our solar system orbits the sun, just as the moon orbits Earth. Our sun is a mighty star. The pull of its gravity is strong. It's so strong that it holds Pluto in orbit from 5.8 billion kilometers (3.6 billion miles) away!

Stars and planets are formed when gravity pulls dust and other small particles together. First, the dust floats as a cloud. When something disturbs the cloud, such as a comet, it starts a **reaction**. Gravity pulls the particles together. As they form small clumps, their mass increases. So, they have more gravity. And more particles are pulled in. The process speeds up. Finally, a star or a planet is formed.

Scientists think there are nearly 100 billion galaxies in our universe.

Black Holes

The planets in our solar system orbit the sun. And our entire solar system is spinning in a large **galaxy**. At the center lies a black hole. A black hole is a place where gravity is so intense that nothing, not even light, can escape its pull. Black holes sometimes form when large stars become unstable. The **matter** in these stars collapses and forms a huge mass at a tiny point in space. A black hole is born.

galaxy

black hole

Gravity turns dust clouds into stars and planets.

solar system

Pulling It All Together

Gravity has been around since time began. It affects everything from time to black holes. And it holds our entire universe together. It may have even created our universe! But there is still much we don't understand about gravity. Scientists are studying it closely and testing new ideas. We may one day live on the moon where there is little gravity. Or we may need to find ways to create gravity. But for now, we need to understand gravity's importance and the many ways it influences our lives.

This is a digital model of what a base on the moon could look like.

Think Like a Scientist

How is gravity's pull related to weight? Experiment and find out!

What to Get

- 1-pound hand weights
- masking tape
- paper and pencil
- ruler

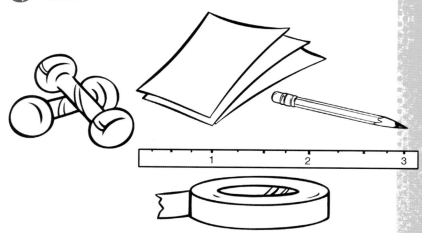

What to Do

1 Tape a ruler to the wall so the bottom touches the floor.

2 Ask a partner to jump three times without holding the weights. (Jumping three times helps avoid strange results that might occur with just one jump.) Record the heights of the jumps in a chart like this one.

	Without Weights	With Weights
Jump 1		
Jump 2		
Jump 3		

3 Next, have your partner jump three times while holding the hand weights. Record the heights of the jumps in the chart.

4 Compare the heights of the jumps. What do you notice about the heights of the jumps with weights versus those without weights?

No Weights   With Weights

Glossary

celestial—of or relating to the sky

evaporates—changes from a liquid into a gas

force—a push or pull on an object

galaxy—a system of stars, gas, and dust held together by gravity

inertia—property of matter in which still objects stay at rest and moving objects keep moving at the same speed in the same direction

matter—anything that has mass and takes up space

orbiting—traveling around something on a curved path

particles—very small pieces of something

reaction—a change that occurs when two or more substances combine

rock cycle—a model that describes the changes rocks go through as a result of Earth's processes

satellites—objects in space that orbit other larger objects

water cycle—a model that describes the changes water goes through, including precipitation, evaporation, and condensation

Index

Gravity at Play

Visit a playground near your school or home. Climb up and down the slide. Climb up, across, and down the monkey bars. Take a ride on the swings. Spin on the merry-go-round. List the ways you feel the effects of gravity.